LIFE'S LITTLE CHERRY COOKBOOK:

101 Cherry Recipes

by Joan Bestwick

Life's Little Cherry Cookbook:
101 Cherry Recipes
by Joan Bestwick

Copyright 2006
by Avery Color Studios, Inc.
ISBN-13: 978-1-892384-38-6
ISBN-10: 1-892384-38-8
Library of Congress Control Number: 2006926786
First Edition 2006
10 9 8 7 6 5 4 3 2 1

Published by
Avery Color Studios, Inc.
Gwinn, Michigan 49841

Cover photo by Michael Prokopowicz
Michael's Photographics, Gwinn, Michigan

Proudly printed in U.S.A.

Table of Contents

First of all I would like to dedicate this book to my Lord and Savior Jesus Christ.

My friends who never get thanked for their hours of serving the Lord endlessly, Patty Cadarette, Jenna Townsend, Connie Howard, Brenda Dault, Paula Thulbult, Annett Brewington, Chris Angle, Glen and Jeanette Manning, Syliva Owens, Pauline Fialkowski, John Ritter, Mike and Jeanie Corneliues, Dale and Karen Sharboneau. You have true Servant hearts.

All the bikers who ride for Jesus, my uncle Harmon and aunt Dee Manning, cousin Carol Jean, Mark Kolnowksi and Jim and Julie Robarge.

*H*ello,

I love cherries. They are my excuse for road trips! I love to travel to the other side of the state to see cherry orchards in blossom. The pinks are breathtaking. Then in the summer to get these sweet morsels. It brings back childhood memories to see the roadside stands where I can get a bag of washed black cherries to munch on in the car. The farmers markets and fruit orchards are where I load up on the cherries to bring home, not to mention if they have my favorite homemade cherry pies, dried cherries and many other food products which are fun to try. When I pit cherries I arm myself with rubber gloves, old clothes, knife, a roll of paper towels and bowls. There has to be an easier way other than buying them frozen. But sometimes working hard for your food is all worth the time. Not only is it worth the taste but you make a family memory. My son loves these trips and it stimulates him in his creativity in the kitchen cooking with me. I hope you make memories in your home with your family cooking.

God bless you,
Joan Bestwick
and Michael too

Cherries

The cherry is a small round, plump fruit with a pit in it. The color can range from a light golden color to a very deep dark red, almost black in color. The skin is shiny and smooth with a long stem. Cherries have a sweet to a sour taste and can be purchased or picked fresh. You can also find them frozen, canned, candied or dried. Maraschino cherries have been preserved and dyed with food coloring. For the dried candied cherries, the red cherries are dyed with red food coloring and almond flavoring and the green cherries have been dyed green with mint flavoring.

Cherry pits have an almond flavor which explains why cherry recipes often use almond extract. This enhances the cherry flavor.

Cherry Varieties

There are two main groups of cherries, sweet or sour.

Sweet cherries, the most popular are the black or gold, which have very little flavor and are mostly used for maraschino cherries and your Queen Anne cherry which is a yellow cherry with pink cheeks.

The best known sour cherry is the Montmorency cherry. It's your good old fashioned cherry.

The Tartarian cherry is just that, a tart cherry.

The Black Balaton cherry is an European cherry. They have the flavor of a tart cherry but the skin of a black cherry.

Cherry Facts

Some of the health benefits of the Montmorency tart cherries are that they are high in vitamin A, beta-carotene and melatonin. They also have strong anti-inflammatory properties. There are 17 components in tart cherries with antioxidant properties and they have a low glycemic index so blood sugars don't spike.

How to buy and store cherries

Cherries can be bought fresh from stores, farmers markets and roadside stands. You can also buy them frozen, canned, candied or dried. Some people will buy the fresh cherries and can, process, freeze or dehydrate them.

Storage

Fresh cherries should be eaten as soon as possible. They can be covered and refrigerated up to 4 days. After opening canned cherries, store in an airtight container in the refrigerator up to 1 week. Maraschino cherries can last up to 6 months in the refrigerator.

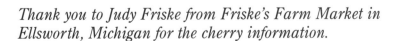

Thank you to Judy Friske from Friske's Farm Market in Ellsworth, Michigan for the cherry information.

APPETIZERS
& BEVERAGES

Be content with what you have.

Blue Cheese Cherry Dip
If you like blue cheese, you'll love this.

1 cup chopped dried cherries
1/2 cup crumbled blue cheese
1/2 cup chopped walnuts or slivered almonds
1 cup sour cream
1/4 cup mayonnaise

In a bowl, stir together all the ingredients mixing well. Chill for at least 2 hours. Serve with cut up vegetables, crackers or bagel slices.

Cherry Cream Cheese Spread

1 3-ounce package cream cheese, softened
1 teaspoon milk
1/8 teaspoon almond extract
1 tablespoon maraschino cherries, chopped

In a small mixing bowl, beat the cream cheese, milk and extract until fluffy. Fold in cherries. Serve with bagels, crackers or toast. Store in refrigerator. Makes 1/3 cup.

Cherry Salsa

1-1/2 cups frozen tart cherries
1/4 cup dried cherries, chopped
1/4 cup red onion, finely chopped
1/2 to 1 tablespoon jalapeno peppers, chopped
1 clove garlic, minced
1 teaspoon cornstarch

Drain frozen tart cherries, reserving the juice and chop. In a saucepan over medium-high heat, mix the cherries, onion, peppers and garlic. Mix well. In a small container, mix 1 tablespoon of the reserved cherry juice and cornstarch until smooth then add to the cherry mixture. Cook and stir constantly until the mixture is thickened. Let cool.

Note: When using jalapeno peppers, cooking them releases the heat. You can always add heat, you can't take it away.

Cherry Crab Dip

1 8-ounce package cream cheese, softened
2 tablespoons milk
1 8-ounce package crab meat, shredded or flaked (if using canned, drain well)
1-2 tablespoons green or red onion, finely diced
1/4 teaspoon seasoned salt
1/2 teaspoon garlic powder
1/8 cup dried cherries, chopped
Optional: parsley, chives, green onion, or nuts, chopped for garnish for the outside of the cheese ball

In a small bowl, beat the cream cheese and milk until fluffy. Stir in the crab meat, onions, seasoned salt and garlic powder, mix well. Stir in the cherries. Move the cheese mixture onto plastic wrap, folding the wrap around the cheese, form into a ball and chill. Carefully unwrap the ball and roll in a garnish if you choose. Then wrap the ball back up in clean plastic wrap or cover on a serving bowl. Serve with crackers - I like celery.

Note: You can use wax paper instead of plastic wrap if you choose.

Cherry Cheese Ball

2 8-ounce packages cream cheese, softened
1/2 cup confectioners sugar
2/3 cup flaked coconut
8-10 maraschino cherries, finely chopped
3/4 cup pecans, finely chopped
Assortment of fruits

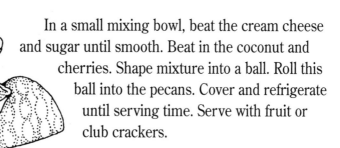

In a small mixing bowl, beat the cream cheese and sugar until smooth. Beat in the coconut and cherries. Shape mixture into a ball. Roll this ball into the pecans. Cover and refrigerate until serving time. Serve with fruit or club crackers.

Cherry Sherbet Smoothies

1-1/2 cups unsweetened apple juice
1 cup frozen unsweetened raspberries
1 cup frozen dark, sweet cherries, pitted
1-1/2 cups raspberry sherbet

In a blender combine the apple juice, raspberries and cherries. Add the sherbet, cover and process until well blended. Pour into chilled glasses. Serve immediately. Makes 4 servings.

JAMS, JELLIES & SAUCES

Live your life as an exclamation not an explanation.

Cherry Peach Jam

1-1/2 cups (1 pound) tart red cherries pitted and chopped
2 cups (1-1/4 pound) peeled and pitted peaches
2 tablespoons lemon juice
1 package powder fruit pectin
4 cups sugar
1 tablespoon margarine

Over medium-high heat, in a heavy kettle, combine the cherries, peaches and lemon juice. Add the fruit pectin and mix well. Bring this mixture to a rolling boil and stir in the sugar. Bring to a full rolling boil again for 1 minute, then add the margarine. Pour in hot sterilized jars and seal. Makes 5 half pints.

Cherry Jam

2 cups cherries, pitted and chopped (I use dark sweet)
4 cups sugar
1 cup water
1 package pectin
1 tablespoon margarine

Mix the fruit and sugar in a bowl. In a heavy pot, boil the pectin and water stirring constantly. Add the fruit and sugar mixture and bring back to a boil. Add the margarine and stir for 1 minute. Pour into hot, sterilized jars and seal.

Cherrapeno Jelly

This recipe was invented by Victoria VanDyke, it's really good.

4 cups canned cherry juice
1/4 cup jalapeno peppers, finely chopped with some juice
1 package fruit pectin
5-1/2 cups sugar

Mix cherry juice, jalapenos with juice and fruit pectin. Place over heat gradually adding sugar, stirring constantly. Bring to a full rolling boil, that can not be stirred down. Continue at a boil for 2 minutes. Remove from heat. Fill jelly jars and seal. Yield is about 6-1/2 cups.

Note: If a milder or hotter jelly is desired, delete or add jalapeno peppers to taste.

Cherry Marmalade

2 oranges
4 cups sweet cherries, pitted
4 tablespoons lemon juice
3-1/2 cups sugar

Wash the oranges, peel them and slice the peel thin. Cover the peel with water and boil for 15 minutes, drain. Chop the pulp of the orange, trying to remove all of the orange membrane. Add enough water in the pan to cover. Boil until soft, cool. Add the cherries, lemon juice and sugar to the oranges. Boil to jelly point or when it thickens. Pour into hot jelly jars and seal.

Cherry Sauce for Filling

3/4 cup sugar
2 tablespoons cornstarch
dash of salt
1/3 cup water
4 cups fresh or frozen tart red cherries, pitted

In a saucepan combine the sugar, cornstarch and salt. Stir in the water and cherries. Cook over medium heat until thick and bubbly. Cook and stir 1 to 2 minutes longer. Cover and chill without stirring. This will make the same quantity as a 21-ounce can of cherry pie filling.

Southwest Cherry Barbecue Sauce

This is from Joel Reeves, who made up this recipe.

1 cup white onions, chopped
2 tablespoons garlic, chopped
2 tablespoons sesame oil
1 cup water
1/2 cup cider vinegar
4 tablespoons ketchup
1/2 cup raspberry jelly, melted

2 tablespoons molasses
1 cup frozen tart cherries
1/4 teaspoon red pepper flakes
1/2 teaspoon ground ginger
2 teaspoons cumin seeds, toasted
1/4 cup brown sugar
1/4 teaspoon chipotle chili powder

Saute onion and garlic in sesame oil, over medium heat, in a large saucepan until onion is translucent. Add all of the remaining ingredients and simmer 30 minutes.

If you like your barbecue sauce "chunky" style, use as is. If you like your barbecue sauce or marinade "smooth," allow sauce to cool and process in food processor. This may be thickened with cornstarch and water if desired. This makes a little more than a quart of sauce.

Cherry Applesauce

1/2 cup sugar
2 tablespoons water
4 medium Rome Beauty apples, peeled, cored and chopped
1-1/2 cups fresh bing cherries, chopped
1/2 teaspoon ground cinnamon
1/2 teaspoon ground ginger
1/2 teaspoon lemon peel, grated

In a large saucepan, heat the sugar and water over medium heat until the sugar is dissolved, stirring occasionally. Stir in the apples, cover and cook for 5 minutes, stirring occasionally. Stir in the cherries and cook another 8-10 minutes. Cover and cook 5 minutes or until the apples are tender. Add cinnamon, ginger and lemon peel. Cook and stir for 5 minutes. Remove from heat. Use a potato masher and mash until you reach your desire consistency.

Spicy Cherry Sauce

We use this for our Christmas ham, awesome.

3/4 cup sugar
2 tablespoons cornstarch
1/2 teaspoon salt
1/3 cup orange juice
1 tablespoon lemon juice
2 cups tart red cherries, pitted (we use home canned)
1/4 teaspoon ground cinnamon
dash of ground cloves

In a medium saucepan, combine about half of the sugar, then add the cornstarch and salt. Stir in the orange and lemon juice. Stir in the undrained cherries, cinnamon and cloves. Cook and stir over medium heat until thickened and bubbly. Cook and stir for 1 to 2 minutes more. Stir in the remaining sugar. Makes about 2 and 2/3 cups.

Cranberry Cherry Relish

1 16-ounce can whole cranberry sauce
1 cup fresh or frozen dark cherries, pitted
1/2 cup raisins
1/4 cup onion, minced
1/4 cup firmly packed brown sugar
2 tablespoons balsamic vinegar
1 tablespoon fresh ginger, minced

Combine all the ingredients in a heavy non-aluminum saucepan. Bring to a boil, reduce heat and simmer uncovered 20 minutes or until thickened. Store in refrigerator. Makes 2-1/2 cups.

Pickled Cherries

My mentor, Rose Kakish says pickled cherries are "it".

24 whole cloves
1 cinnamon stick
2 quarts sour or black cherries with pits and stems
2-1/4 cups vinegar
4 tablespoons sugar

Make spice bag out of cloves and cinnamon. In a medium saucepan mix the sugar and vinegar. Add the spices and cook for 5 minutes. Add the cherries and cook slowly until they are tender. Let stand overnight. Remove the spice bag. Place cherries in hot sterilized jars. Boil reserved spicy syrup until it thickens slightly. Pour hot over cherries. Seal and process.

Rose said she dips her cherries in raw sugar. This is a great compliment to pork roast.

BREAKFAST FAVORITES

What you did is not important.
What you learned from it is.

Easy Cherry Pancakes

1-1/4 cups all-purpose flour
2 tablespoons granulated sugar
2 teaspoons baking powder
1/2 teaspoon salt
1 beaten egg
1 cup milk
1 tablespoon cooking oil
1/2 cup black cherries, chopped

In a bowl, stir together the flour, sugar, baking powder and salt. Combine the egg, milk and oil in a separate bowl. Add the wet ingredients to the dry ingredients and stir until well blended. The batter will be slightly lumpy. Fold in the cherries. On a hot griddle, ladle the batter onto the hot surface, about 1/4 cup per pancake. Cook until the edges of the pancake are bubbly and the batter is starting to set. Flip the pancake and cook until golden brown on both sides.

For a short cut on this recipe, you can use your favorite pancake mix and mix according to directions and add the cherries.

Cherry Steel Cut Oatmeal

This recipe is from my cool mom Maryanne Manning.

1 cup Steel Cut oats
1/2 cup dried tart cherries
2 teaspoons finely shredded orange peel
1/4 teaspoon ground cinnamon
1/8 teaspoon salt
dash of ground nutmeg
2 cups milk
2 tablespoons butter
1-1/2 tablespoons sugar
1/4 cup chopped walnuts

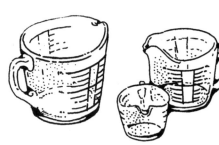

In a glass or plastic bowl combine the oats, cherries, orange peel, cinnamon, salt and nutmeg. Stir in the milk, cover and chill for 8 to 24 hours. To cook, place the oatmeal mixture into a medium saucepan. Heat to a boil, reduce heat. Simmer uncovered for 5 minutes or until the oatmeal is done, stirring occasionally. Remove from heat. Stir in the butter until melted. If desired add more milk to desired consistency. Serve in a bowl topped with sugar and nuts.

Cherry Maple Syrup Granola

4 cups rolled oats
1 cup walnuts, almonds, or pecans (your preference), chopped
1 cup coconut
1/2 teaspoon salt
1/4 cup maple syrup
1/4 cup oil
1 cup dried cherries

Preheat oven to 375°. In a bowl, mix the oats, nuts, coconut and salt. Mix the maple syrup and oil together, then add this to the oat mixture. Mix well. Spread mixture on a large cookie sheet and bake for about 40 minutes, stirring often. Add the cherries after granola has been removed from the oven. Cool and store in an airtight container.

Easy Cherry-Blueberry Pancakes

Your favorite pancake batter
1/4 cup black, sweet cherries, chopped
1/4 cup blueberries

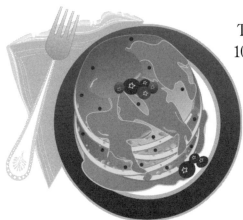

Take you pancake batter and mix up a 10-12 quantity batch. Add the cherries and blueberries to the batter and cook per package directions. Serve with warm syrup. This is awesome.

Black Cherry Syrup

2 cups black cherries, pitted and chopped
1/2 cup sugar, adjust to taste and sweetness of cherries
1/2 cup or so of water
1 teaspoon vanilla extract

In a saucepan, place the black cherries, sugar and water. Bring to a boil and cook down to the consistency you desire. Adjust the sugar, I have used Splenda® with the same results as granulated sugar. Add vanilla at the end of cooking. This is very good over pancakes or angel food cake.

SALADS

*Share the gift of food
with those less fortunate.*

Cherry Chicken Salad

1 cup fresh orange juice
1/2 cup dried cherries
4 cups cooked chicken, chopped
1/3 cup mayonnaise
1/4 cup sour cream
2 teaspoons fresh tarragon
1 teaspoon orange rind, grated
1/2 teaspoon salt
1/4 teaspoon pepper
crackers

In a small saucepan, bring the juice and cherries to a boil over medium-high heat. Reduce the heat and simmer 10-12 minutes or until the liquid is reduced to a 1/4 cup. Remove from heat and cool slightly. Pour the mixture into a large bowl. Stir in the chicken and the next six ingredients. Mix well and chill for at least 2 hours so the flavors meld. Serve with crackers.

Feta Cheese Waldorf Salad

2 medium apples, unpeeled, cored and cubed
2 tablespoons lemon juice
1 cup dried cherries
1 cup celery, sliced
1/2 cup mayonnaise
1/2 cup walnuts, chopped
2 to 3 tablespoons feta cheese, crumbled

In a medium bowl, toss the apple and lemon juice. Combine the rest of the ingredients and incorporate well. Chill for a couple of hours. Serve.

Cherry-Apple Salad

2 cups apple juice
1 6-ounce package cherry flavored gelatin
2 cups dark sweet cherries, frozen or canned, pitted
1/2 cup celery, thinly sliced
1/2 cup walnuts, chopped
1 3-ounce package cream cheese, softened
1 cup applesauce

In a saucepan, bring the apple juice to a boil. In a bowl, add the juice and gelatin, stirring until dissolved. If using canned cherries reserve the cherry juice. Cut the cherries in half or quarters and set aside. Stir in 1-1/2 cups of liquid (water and if there is reserved juice) into the gelatin and set aside two cups of the gelatin mixture at room temperature. Chill remaining gelatin until partially set. To this, fold in the cherries, celery and walnuts. Pour this into a 6-1/2 cup ring mold. Chill until almost firm. In a mixing bowl, beat the reserved room temperature gelatin with the softened cream cheese, beating until smooth. Stir in the applesauce and spoon over the top of the cherry mixture in the mold. Chill until firm. Unmold and serve.

Cherry Broccoli Salad

This is a take off from the Apple Broccoli Salad from the
Life's Little Apple Cookbook.

3 cups broccoli flowerets
1-1/4 cups swiss cheese, shredded
1 cup dried tart cherries
3/4 cup dry roasted sunflower seeds
1/2 cup red onions, chopped
1/2 cup mayonnaise
1/2 cup plain yogurt or sour cream
2 tablespoons raspberry vinaigrette
1/4 pound bacon, fried crisp, crumbled

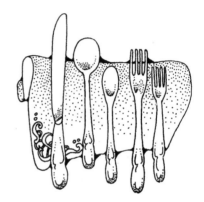

In a large mixing bowl, combine the first 5 ingredients. In a small bowl, combine the next 3 ingredients until well incorporated. Pour the dressing ingredients over the broccoli mixture and fold until well mixed. Sprinkle the bacon over the top, cover and chill. Stir before serving. Makes 8 to 12 servings.

Frozen Party Salad

1 cup Miracle Whip® salad dressing
8 ounce cream cheese
1 cup pineapple chunks
1 can fruit cocktail
1/2 cup maraschino cherries
2 cups miniature marshmallows
1 cup whipping cream

In a bowl, blend the cream cheese with the salad dressing. Fold in the pineapple, fruit cocktail, cherries and marshmallows. In a separate bowl, whip the cream until fluffy and then fold into the fruit mixture. Place paper baking cups into muffin tins. Fill cups with salad and put into freezer. Let set at room temperature for a few minutes before serving.

Cream Cheese Salad

1 pound (16 ounces) marshmallows
1/2 cup milk
3 3-ounce packages cream cheese
1 pint cottage cheese
1 16-ounce can crushed pineapple, drained
1/2 cup chopped nuts
1 small jar maraschino cherries, cut up
1 8-ounce container whipped topping

Melt marshmallows in the milk in a double boiler. Then add cream cheese and cottage cheese. Stir until melted. Cool a little, then add pineapple, chopped nuts and cherries. Chill 30 minutes and fold in the whipped topping. Let set.

Feta Walnut Salad

1 5-ounce package mixed salad greens
1 cup dried cherries
1/2 cup feta cheese, crumbled
1/2 cup toasted walnuts, chopped
1 teaspoon dijon mustard
2 tablespoons balsamic vinegar
2 tablespoons honey
1/4 cup olive oil

In a large bowl, toss the salad greens, cherries, feta and walnuts until mixed. In a small bowl with a whisk, mix the mustard, vinegar and honey until blended. Gradually add the oil, whisking until well combined. Pour over the salad to toss and coat. Serves 4 to 6 people.

Cherry Jello® Salad

1 15-ounce can dark sweet cherries, pitted
1 11-ounce can mandarin oranges
1 8-ounce can crushed pineapple
1 6-ounce package cherry flavored Jello®
1 cup cold water
1/2 cup pecans, chopped

Drain all canned fruit into a bowl reserving the juice. Set the fruit aside. Bring the reserved fruit juice to a boil in a saucepan. Add the gelatin and cook, stirring constantly for 2 minutes or until gelatin dissolves. Remove from heat. Stir in the cold water and chill until thickened. Fold in the drained fruit and pecans. Pour into mold if desired. Chill until set. Serves 8 to 10.

Spinach Salad

1/3 cup olive oil
3 tablespoons sugar
2 tablespoons white wine vinegar
2 tablespoons sour cream
1/2 teaspoon ground mustard
1 6-ounce package fresh baby spinach
1/2 cup toasted walnuts, chopped
1/2 cup dried cherries
1 small can mandarin oranges, drained

In a container that has a tight fitting lid, combine the first 5 ingredients. Shake well. In a salad bowl, place the spinach leaves and drizzle with the salad dressing. Sprinkle with walnuts, cherries and oranges. Serves 4.

Frozen Fruit Salad

1 16-ounce can dark sweet cherries, pitted and drained
1 15 1/4-ounce can pineapple chunks, drained
1/2 cup toasted pecans, chopped
1 12-ounce container whipped topping
1 8-ounce carton lemon yogurt
1/2 cup mayonnaise

In a large bowl, combine the cherries, pineapple and pecans. Then in a separate bowl, combine the whipped topping, yogurt and mayonnaise. Fold this mixture into the fruit mixture. When this is blended, spoon into a 11 x 7 inch dish. Cover and freeze at least 8 hours or until firm. To serve cut the frozen salad into squares and serve on lettuce leaves if desired. Serves 8.

SIDE & MAIN DISHES

*All things are possible to him
that believes.* Mark 9:23

Cherry Candied Sweet Potatoes

1 large can sweet potatoes
1 cup frozen tart cherries
3 tablespoons maple syrup
1/4 cup brown sugar
1/2 cup butter or margarine, melted
1/2 teaspoon nutmeg
1/4 teaspoon ground ginger

In a 1-1/2 quart baking dish, place the sweet potatoes. Sprinkle the cherries over the sweet potatoes. Combine the maple syrup, brown sugar, margarine, nutmeg and ginger. Pour this mixture over the potatoes and bake at 350° for 30-40 minutes, or until hot and bubbly.

Dried Fruit Wild Rice Dressing

1 6-ounce package long grain and wild rice mix
6 cups country style bread, cut in 1/2-inch cubes
1 pound ground pork sausage
2 small onions, chopped
4 celery ribs, chopped
1/4 cup butter
1 cup dried apricots, coarsely chopped
3/4 cup dried cherries
1/2 cup fresh parsley, chopped
1/2 teaspoon salt
1/2 teaspoon pepper
1 cup chicken broth

Prepare the rice mix according to the package directions. Transfer to a large bowl and fluff the rice with a fork, set aside.

Meanwhile, place the bread cubes on a large pan and toast at 325° for 20 minutes or until dry. Set aside. Cook

Dried Fruit Wild Rice Dressing *Continued*

sausage in a large skillet over medium heat, stirring until crumbled and browned. Drain on a paper towel. Saute onion and celery in butter in a large skillet over medium heat until tender.

Combine the rice, bread, sausage, sauteed vegetables, dried fruit, parsley, salt and pepper in a large bowl. Mix well. Drizzle broth evenly over the dressing. Toss well. Transfer dressing to a lightly greased 3 quart bake dish. Bake covered at 375° for 20 minutes. Uncover and bake for 25 to 30 minutes or until browned. Makes 8 to 10 servings.

Cherry Stuffing

2 tablespoons butter or margarine
1-1/2 cups celery, chopped
3/4 cup onion, chopped
7 ounces dried bread cubes
1-3/4 cups chicken broth
2 teaspoons poultry seasoning
1/4 teaspoon salt
pepper to taste
1/2 cup dried cherries

In a saucepan melt butter and saute the celery and onion until tender. In a bowl combine the bread cubes, broth and seasonings. Add the onion, celery and cherries and mix well. You can stuff poultry or pork with this stuffing.

Sweet Cherries and Chicken

2-1/2 to 3 pounds chicken legs, skinned
1 teaspoon poultry seasoning
1 15 to 17-ounce can dark sweet cherries, pitted
1 12-ounce bottle chili sauce
1/2 cup packed brown sugar

Place the chicken into a crockpot and sprinkle with the poultry seasoning. In a medium bowl, combine the cherries, chili sauce and brown sugar. Pour this mixture over the chicken. Cover and cook on low heat for 5 to 6 hours or high heat for about 3 hours. Each crockpot is different, these are estimated times. To serve, transfer the chicken to plates and spoon some sauce over it. Good with white rice. Serves 4.

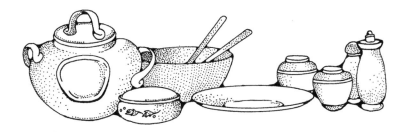

Joel's Cherry Shrimp In Butter Sauce

This is from Joel Reeves. He's in culinary school and is one of my best friend's son.

2 tablespoons olive oil
1 tablespoon garlic, minced
1 tablespoon shallot, finely chopped
1 teaspoon lemon juice
5 large shrimp or prawn, thawed
1/4 cup green onion, chopped
3 tablespoons bacon, cooked
   and crumbled

1 cup baby leaf spinach, cleaned,
   drained and chopped
3 tablespoons dried cherries, may
   substitute frozen
1/2 cup apple juice
1/4 cup whole butter, room
   temperature
salt and pepper to taste

Heat olive oil in a skillet over medium heat. Add the garlic, shallot and lemon juice. Saute the shrimp in this mixture until it is pink on both sides, do not allow garlic to brown. Add the green onions, bacon, spinach, cherries and apple juice. Cook over medium heat until the liquid is reduced by half. Take the pan from the heat and allow the pan to cool (to approximately 140°) before adding the butter (butter will "break" at high temperatures). Using a large spoon, slowly stir in butter to create an emulsion with the juice. Stir in all of the butter until the sauce is creamy. Add salt and pepper to taste.

Serving size: 1 portion. Serving suggestions: This may be served plain as an appetizer. Add grits or rice to the plate to make an entree portion.

Pork Roast With Cherry Sauce

1 3 to 4 pound pork roast
1 teaspoon salt
1 teaspoon pepper
1 teaspoon sage
1 16-ounce can tart cherries
1-1/2 cups sugar

1/4 cup vinegar
8 whole cloves
1 stick cinnamon
1/3 cup cornstarch
1 tablespoon lemon juice
1-2 tablespoons butter or margarine

Preheat oven to 325°. Take your roast and rub it down with the salt, pepper and sage. Bake uncovered for 1-1/2 to 2 hours until done. While the roast is cooking, drain your cherries and reserve the juice. You will need 3/4 cup liquid, so add water to the juice to measure 3/4 cup. In a saucepan, pour 1/2 cup of the juice into the pan. Add the sugar, vinegar, cloves and cinnamon stick. In a small bowl, combine the remaining juice and cornstarch, whisk until smooth. Add this to the saucepan and bring to a boil, cook until thickened stirring constantly. Stir in lemon juice, butter and cherries. Heat through. Let roast stand so juices can redistribute. Slice and serve with cherry sauce.

Cherry Beef Stir Fry

3/4 pound beef steak, thinly sliced
1-1/2 cups frozen tart cherries,
    thawed, reserving the juice
1/3 cup soy sauce
1/4 cup vegetable oil
3 tablespoons honey
1/2 teaspoon ground ginger
1 clove garlic, minced
1 tablespoon cornstarch

1 tablespoon oil
1 small package pea pods
1 small zucchini, sliced thin
    or julienned
1 bunch green onions, sliced
1 can water chestnuts, drained
    and sliced
hot cooked rice

In a shallow dish, combine the soy sauce, oil, honey, ginger and garlic. Add the beef strips and coat. Refrigerate for 1 hour covered to marinate. Remove the meat from the marinade. Take the reserved cherry juice and measure 1/4 cup, adding water if needed. Stir in the cornstarch and mix well.

In a skillet over medium heat, add 1 tablespoon oil, when hot add the pea pods, zucchini and onions. Cook until crisp tender. Remove the vegetables to a bowl. Add more oil if needed and the meat, cook until done then remove from the pan. Add the cornstarch mixture to the pan and cook until thickened and bubbly, stirring constantly. Add the vegetables, meat, cherries and water chestnuts. Heat for about 5 minutes. Serve over hot rice.

Grilled Chicken With Cherry Peach Sauce

4 skinless, boneless chicken breast
1 can peach slices, drained, reserving juice
1 tablespoon red wine vinegar
1 tablespoon brown sugar
1 tablespoon Dijon mustard
1 cup dried cherries

Grill your chicken breast or cook as desired. In a large frying pan, combine 1-1/2 cups reserved peach juice (adding water to make 1-1/2 cups if needed), vinegar, brown sugar and mustard. Mix well. Add the dried cherries and bring to a boil, reduce heat and simmer for 10 minutes. Add the peach slices and simmer until the sauce thickens, about 5 minutes. Serve the sauce over the chicken.

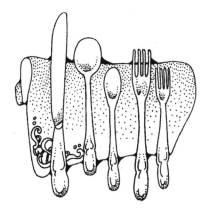

Duck In Cherry Sauce

4 to 5 pound duckling
2 unpeeled oranges, quartered
1 clove of garlic, chopped
1 teaspoon salt
crack black pepper or 3 whole peppers
1/2 cup butter or margarine, melted
1 cup apple or white grape juice
1 1-pound can pitted dark sweet cherries, or frozen, drained
1 clove garlic, very finely chopped
1/4 cup onion, finely chopped
1/4 cup unsifted all-purpose flour
2 teaspoons beef bouillon
1-1/4 cups canned chicken broth
1/4 cup currant jelly

Preheat oven to 425°. Take your duckling and stuff the cavity with orange quarters, chopped garlic, salt and peppers. Truss the bird (tie the legs together with cotton string). Place the duckling breast side up on the rack in a roasting pan. Brush the top well with the melted butter. Roast uncovered for 30 minutes. Reduce the oven to 375° and roast for 1-1/2 hours. Drain the fat as

Duck In Cherry Sauce *Continued*

it accumulates. In a bowl, pour the juice over the cherries and let stand for about 1 hour. When the duck is almost done, make the sauce. Pour 1/4 cup of the pan drippings from the duck into a medium saucepan. Saute in a pan the garlic and onion in some of the pan drippings. Remove from heat and stir in the flour, bouillon until smooth. Then whisk in the broth bringing to a boil. Blend in the cherries in the juice and jelly until the jelly melts and the sauce is heated through.

When the duckling is done, remove the cotton string. Place on a platter and carve, pour some of the sauce over the poultry. Serve the cherry sauce as your gravy. Very good! Serves about 4 people.

Tip: When duck is removed from oven, cover with foil and let stand 10-15 minutes so the juices can redistribute.

Pork Tenderloin With Cherry And Mango Salsa

From my first cousin, Chef Amy Denstedt.

Salsa:
2 mangos, peeled and diced
1/4 cup fresh cherries, preferably tart
1/4 cup red bell pepper, chopped
3 scallions, bottoms and 2 inches
   of green, thinly sliced
juice of one lime
1 teaspoon light brown sugar

Tenderloin:
1 tenderloin
1 cup of dried cherries
1 cup of white grape juice
1 cup of water

Mix diced fruits and vegetables together in a bowl. Squeeze the lime over the fruit and vegetables and sprinkle with the sugar. Stir until well blended and refrigerate until ready for use.

In a saucepan, combine the cherries, juice and water. Bring to a boil and reduce to a thin sauce. Place tenderloin in a shallow pan, pouring sauce over the meat and bake at 350° until well done. With a ladle, occasionally pour some of the sauce over the tenderloin to reintroduce the flavor onto the meat. Add salt and pepper to taste.

When the tenderloin is cooked to well done, remove from the oven and let it sit for about 5-10 minutes. Then thinly slice the meat and fan it onto the plate, garnishing the tenderloin with the salsa.

Cherry Chicken

6 to 8 chicken breasts, deboned
salt and pepper
dash garlic salt
1 can sour cherries, drained, reserve juice
1/2 cup sugar
1/2 cup reserved cherry juice
1 tablespoon flour
dash of salt
1 orange, peeled, sectioned and membranes removed
1/2 cup sliced or slivered almonds
1/3 cup grape juice

Preheat oven to 400°. Place the chicken breasts in a pan and season with salt, pepper and garlic salt. Bake for 25 minutes. While the chicken bakes, place the cherries into a saucepan and add the sugar. In a small bowl, whisk the cherry juice and flour. Mix this into the cherries with a dash of salt. Heat this mixture until it thickens, then add the orange, almonds and grape juice. Place the cooked chicken in the sauce and simmer 5 minutes or until hot. Serve over white rice.

Pork Chops With Fruit Compote

1 cup dried apple slices
3/4 cup prunes
1/2 cup dried apricots
1/2 cup dried sour cherries
1 cinnamon stick
2 cups fresh orange juice
1 cup white grape juice
4 large pork chops
salt and pepper

To make the dried fruit compote, combine the first 7 ingredients in a large sauce pan. Bring this to a boil and then simmer until the fruit becomes soft, about 30 minutes. Remove the cinnamon stick.

Cook the pork chops until done in a frying pan. Remove to a plate and serve with the compote.

CRISPS, COBBLERS
& BREADS

*A good memory is fine, but the ability to forgive
and forget is the true test of greatness.*

Cherry Nut Crisp

2 14-1/2-ounce cans pitted tart cherries
1 cup sugar
1/4 cup quick cooking tapioca
1 teaspoon almond extract
1/8 teaspoon salt
4 to 5 drops red food coloring (optional)

Crust:
1 cup all-purpose flour
1/3 cup sugar
1/4 teaspoon salt
1/8 teaspoon baking powder
6 tablespoons butter or margarine, melted

Topping:
1/2 cup all-purpose flour
1/2 cup packed brown sugar
1/2 cup chopped pecans, walnuts
    or slivered almonds
1/3 cup quick cooking oats
6 tablespoons color butter or
    margarine

Drain the cherries, reserving 3/4 cup juice. In a bowl combine cherries, sugar, tapioca, extract, salt, food coloring and reserved juice, set aside for 15 minutes stirring occasionally. Combine the crust ingredients and press into a 9-inch square baking dish, set aside. In another bowl combine the first four topping ingredients, cut in the butter until it resembles coarse crumbs. Stir cherry mixture and pour into the crust. Sprinkle with topping and bake at 400° for ten minutes. Reduce heat to 375° and bake 30-35 minutes longer or until filling is bubbly and topping is golden. Makes 9 servings.

Cherry Pineapple Crisp

2 16-ounce cans pitted tart cherries
1 20-ounce can crushed pineapple, undrained
1 cup sugar
1 tablespoon tapioca
1/2 cup quick cooking rolled oats
1/2 cup packed brown sugar
1/4 cup all-purpose flour
1/2 teaspoon ground cinnamon
1/2 teaspoon salt
1-1/2 teaspoons vanilla extract
1/4 cup butter or margarine
ice cream

Drain the cherries reserving 1/3 cup juice. Place the juice in a saucepan. Add the pineapple, sugar and tapioca. Let stand for 5 minutes. In a bowl, combine oats, brown sugar, flour, cinnamon and salt. Mix well. Add the vanilla and toss. Cut the butter into the oat mixture until it crumbles. Press half of the mixture into a greased 13 x 9 x 2 inch baking pan. Bring the cherry mixture to a boil, stirring occasionally. Cook and stir for 1 minute or until thick and bubbly. Pour over the crust. Sprinkle with remaining oat mixture. Bake at 375° for 25 to 30 minutes or until filling is bubbly and the top is golden brown. Serve with ice cream. Serves 12.

Cherry Cobbler

4 cups fresh or frozen pitted
   tart red cherries
3/4 cup sugar
1 tablespoon quick cooking tapioca
1/3 cup water
1 tablespoon butter or margarine
1 cup all-purpose flour

2 tablespoons sugar
1-1/2 teaspoons baking powder
1/4 teaspoon salt
1/4 cup butter or margarine
1 egg, slightly beaten
1/4 cup milk

For the cherry filling: In a medium saucepan, combine the cherries, 3/4 cup sugar, tapioca and water. Let stand 5 minutes, stirring occasionally. Cook this mixture over medium heat until it is thickened and boiling. Set aside and keep warm.

For the topping: Stir together the 1 cup flour, 2 tablespoons sugar, baking powder and salt. With a fork or pastry blender, cut in the 1/4 cup butter or margarine until the mixture resembles coarse crumbs. Combine the beaten egg and milk, then add to the dry ingredients, stirring just until moistened.

In an 8 x 1-1/2 inch round baking dish or a 1-1/2 quart casserole dish, add the hot fruit filling. Spoon the topping onto the fruit in 8 mounds. Bake at 400° for 20 minutes. Serve with ice cream or whipped topping. Serves 6 people.

Quick Cobbler

1 quart black cherries, pitted (or your favorite)
1/2 cup sugar
1 tablespoon flour
2 eggs, beaten
1/2 cup butter or margarine, melted
1/4 teaspoon salt
1-1/2 cups flour
3/4 cup milk
1 cup sugar
1 teaspoon vanilla
2 teaspoons baking powder

Preheat oven to 350°. Put fruit in a cake pan, add 1/2 cup sugar mixed with 1 tablespoon flour. Mix remaining ingredients together and pour evenly over the fruit mixture. Bake for 45 minutes.

Old Fruit Crunch
This is a great grandmother's recipe.

1 can cherry pie filling (large)
1 cup flour
1 cup sugar
1/2 teaspoon salt
2 teaspoons baking powder
2 tablespoons butter
1 egg, beaten

Pour the cherry pie filling into a 9 x 13 inch pan. Mix remaining ingredients in order into a bowl. Dough will be thick and sticky. Bake at 350° for 30 minutes or until top is brown. Serve warm with milk.

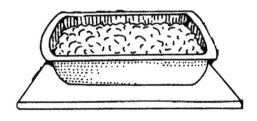

Mom's Banana Cherry Bread

I love this recipe of my Mom's. She always gives me a loaf.

1-3/4 cups all-purpose flour
1-3/4 cups whole wheat flour
2/3 cup white sugar
2/3 cup brown sugar
1 teaspoon salt
1/2 teaspoon baking soda
1 cup shortening
2 cups mashed bananas (4 very ripe)
4 eggs, slightly beaten
1-1/2 cups walnuts, chopped
2 tablespoons flax seeds
1/2 cup sunflower seeds
1-1/2 cups dried cherries (more or less)

Preheat the oven to 350°. Grease and flour three 9 x 5 loaf pans. In a large bowl, with a fork, mix the first six ingredients. With a pastry blender, cut in the shortening until the mixture resembles coarse crumbs. Stir in the bananas and eggs until just blended, add the walnuts, flax seed, sunflower seeds and dried cherries. Mix until just blended. Bake 55 minutes to 1 hour, until toothpick comes out clean. Cool 10 minutes. Remove from pans, cool completely. These freeze well. I use Splenda® sugar and Splenda® brown sugar.

Almond Cherry Nut Bread

2-1/2 cups all-purpose flour
1/2 cup granulated sugar
1/2 cup packed brown sugar
3-1/2 teaspoons baking powder
1/2 teaspoon salt
1 large egg
1-1/4 cups milk or buttermilk
3 tablespoons cooking oil
1/2 teaspoon almond extract
1-1/4 cups maraschino cherries, coarsely chopped
1 cup almonds, coarsely chopped

Preheat oven to 350°. Grease a 9 x 5 x 3 inch loaf pan. In a large bowl, stir the flour, sugars, baking powder and salt. In a small bowl, mix the egg, milk, oil and extract until beat well. Add the wet ingredients to the dry ingredients and mix until moistened. Fold in the cherries and nuts until mixed. Pour batter into the loaf pan and bake for 1 hour or until a wooden toothpick comes out clean. Let the loaf rest in pan for 10 minutes before removing to cool on a wire rack. Makes 1 loaf.

Cherry Pecan Bread

2 cups all-purpose flour
1 teaspoon baking soda
1/2 teaspoon salt
3/4 cup sugar
1/2 cup butter or margarine
2 eggs
1 teaspoon vanilla
1 cup buttermilk or sour milk
1 cup pecans, chopped
1 cup maraschino cherries, chopped

Preheat oven to 350°. Grease a 9 x 5 x 3 inch loaf pan. In a mixing bowl, stir together the flour, soda and salt. Set aside. In a large mixing bowl, beat together the sugar and butter until creamed, add the eggs one at a time along with the vanilla. Add the flour mixture and milk alternately, beating into the sugar mixture until blended. Fold in the nuts and cherries. Turn this mixture into the loaf pan and bake 55 to 60 minutes. Cool in pan for 10 minutes and then remove from pan. Cool on wire rack. Makes 1 loaf.

Cherry Bread

This recipe is from my favorite uncle - Harmon Manning.

3/4 cup plus 2 tablespoons (7-ounces) water
1-1/2 tablespoons olive oil
1-1/2 tablespoons honey or maple syrup
grated zest of 1 lemon or 1/4 teaspoon dried lemon peel
3 tablespoons cherry jam or all-fruit spread
2-1/2 cups (12-ounces) unbleached all-purpose flour
3/4 cup (3-1/2 ounces) whole wheat flour
2 tablespoons powdered milk
1-1/2 teaspoons salt
2-1/2 teaspoons active dry yeast
1/2 cup (1-1/2 ounces) dried cherries

Put all the ingredients except the dried cherries in the inner pan of your bread machine in the order listed. Select the dough setting and push start. Add the dried cherries when the machine beeps, about 7 minutes after starting. Take the dough out about 30 minutes into the cycle. Roll it out on a flour surface in jelly roll fashion. Place in a greased bread pan and cover with a damp cloth. Let rise in a warm place until double in size, about an hour. Bake it in a 350° preheated oven for 25 to 30 minutes. Remove from oven, remove from pan and place on a wire rack to cool. While still warm, coat the bread with a small amount of margarine.

CAKES & PIES

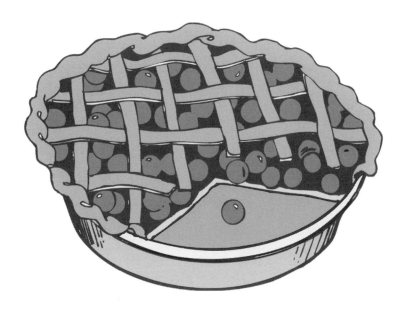

*Live your life in the manner that you would
like your children to live theirs.*

Cherry Coffee Cake

From my mom, Maryanne Manning.

1-1/4 cup all-purpose flour
1/2 cup sugar
1 teaspoon baking powder
1/4 teaspoon baking soda
1/4 teaspoon salt
1/2 cup butter or
   margarine, melted
1/2 cup milk

1 egg
1 teaspoon vanilla
1/2 cup flour
1/4 cup brown sugar
2 tablespoons butter or margarine
1/4 teaspoon lemon or almond
   extract
1 21-ounce can cherry pie filling

Preheat oven to 350°. Grease and flour a 9 x 9 baking pan. In a large bowl with a fork, mix 1-1/4 cup flour with, 1/2 cup sugar, baking powder, baking soda and salt. Add 1/2 cup melted butter or margarine, milk, egg and vanilla. With a spoon, beat until mixed. Pour batter evenly in baking pan. In a small bowl, combine 1/2 cup flour, brown sugar and 2 tablespoons butter or margarine until mixture resembles coarse crumbs. Sprinkle 1/2 on top of the batter. Stir lemon or almond extract into the cherry pie filling. Spread this over the batter and sprinkle with the rest of the flour crumb mixture. Bake 1 hour or until the top is light golden brown. Makes 9 servings.

Note: You can use Splenda® granule brown sugar blend. Also no sugar cherry pie filling sweetened with Splenda®.

Black Forest Cheesecake

1 8-ounce package cream cheese
1/3 cup sugar
1 cup (8-ounces) sour cream
2 teaspoons vanilla extract
1 8-ounce carton whipped topping
1 8-inch chocolate crumb crust
1/4 cup baking cocoa
1 tablespoon confectioners sugar
1 21-ounce can cherry pie filling

In a large mixing bowl, beat the cream cheese and sugar until smooth. Beat in the sour cream and vanilla. Fold in the whipped topping. Spread 1/2 of the mixture evenly into the crust. Fold cocoa and confectioners sugar into remaining whipped topping mixture. Spread this over the cream cheese layer. Refrigerate for at least 4 hours. To serve, cut into slices and top with cherry pie filling.

Cherry Topped Pound Cake

1 package pound cake, frozen cut into 10 slices
1 21-ounce can cherry pie filling
1 12-ounce tub whipped topping
1 cup shredded coconut - optional

Line the bottom of a 12 x 8 inch baking dish with pound cake slices. Top the pound cake with pie filling, then top the cherries with the whipped topping. Chill for 1 hour or until ready to serve. Top with coconut if desired.

Cherry Pudding Cake

2 cups all-purpose flour
2-1/2 cups sugar, divided
4 teaspoons baking powder
1 cup milk
2 tablespoons vegetable oil
2 cans (14-ounces each) water packed, pitted tart red cherries, well drained
2 to 3 drops red food coloring, optional
1/8 teaspoon almond extract
ice cream or whipped topping

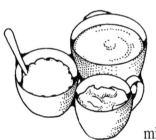

In a mixing bowl, combine flour, 1 cup sugar, baking powder, milk and oil. Pour into a greased shallow 3 quart baking dish. In a bowl, combine cherries, food coloring, extract and remaining sugar. Spoon this over the batter. Bake at 375° for 40-45 minutes or until a wooden toothpick inserted in the cake portion comes out clean. Serve warm with ice cream or whipped topping. Serves 10-12.

Cherry Chocolate Cake

From my friends, Karen and Dan Frampton.

1 Devils Food cake mix
1 21-ounce can cherry pie filling
1 teaspoon almond extract
2 eggs, lightly beaten

Mix all ingredients together. Pour into a greased 9 x 13 inch pan. Bake for 25-30 minutes. Very simple, but delicious!

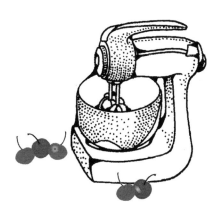

Fruit Cake

1-1/2 cups dates
1 pound candied pineapple
1 pound candied cherries
4 eggs
1 cup sugar
2 cups flour
2 teaspoons baking powder
1/2 teaspoon salt
2 pounds pecans

In a large bowl, mix the dates, pineapple and cherries. Beat the eggs and sugar and then add this to the fruit. Sift together in a bowl, the flour, baking powder and salt. Mix this well with the fruit. Add the pecans and mix well. Grease a bread pan and line with wax paper. Grease the wax paper. Bake for 1-1/2 hours at 275°. Cool 5 minutes and peel the wax paper off the loaf.

Coconut Cherry Cheese Coffee Cake

2-1/2 cups all-purpose flour
3/4 cup sugar
1/2 teaspoon baking powder
1/2 teaspoon baking soda
2 packages (3-ounces each) cream
cheese, divided
3/4 cup milk

2 tablespoons vegetable oil
2 eggs
1 teaspoon vanilla extract
1/2 cup flaked coconut
3/4 cup cherry preserves
2 tablespoons butter

Preheat oven to 350°. Grease and flour a 9-inch spring form pan. Combine flour and sugar in a large bowl. Reserve 1/2 cup of the flour mixture. Stir baking powder and soda into the remaining flour mixture. Cut in 1 package of the cream cheese until mixture resembles coarse crumbs. Set aside. Combine milk, oil and one egg in a medium bowl. Add to cream cheese mixture. Stir just until moistened. Spread batter on bottom and 1-inch up the side of the pan. Blend remaining package of cream cheese, egg and vanilla in a small bowl until smooth. Pour over batter, spreading within one inch of the edge. Sprinkle with coconut, spoon preserves evenly over the top. Cut butter into reserved flour mixture until it resembles coarse crumbs. Sprinkle over the preserves. Bake for 55 to 60 minutes or until toothpick inserted into crust comes out clean. Cool in pan on wire rack for 15 minutes. Remove sides of pan. Serve warm. Makes 10 servings.

Almond Cherry Pie

4 cups tart red cherries, pitted
3/4 cup sugar
1 tablespoon butter or margarine
dash of salt
1/4 cup cornstarch
1/3 cup cold water
1/2 teaspoon almond extract
pastry for a double crust 9-inch pie

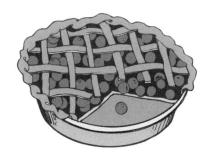

In a bowl, drain the cherries reserving 2/3 cup juice. Transfer the juice to a saucepan, add the cherries, sugar, butter and salt. In a bowl, dissolve the cornstarch in water, then stir this into the cherry mixture. Bring this to a boil over medium heat. Cook and stir until thick and bubbly. Cook and stir 1 minute more, then remove from heat. Stir in the extract and cool. Place bottom pastry in a 9-inch pie plate. Add the filling and top with the remaining pie crust. Cut slits into the top crust for vents. Bake at 375° for 40 to 50 minutes or until crust is golden brown and filling is bubbly. Before baking pie, place on a tin foil topped pizza pan to help prevent a mess in your oven for easy clean up.

Cream Cherry Crumb Pie

1/2 cup sugar
3 tablespoons all-purpose flour
2 15-ounce cans tart cherries,
    pitted and drained
1 cup (8-ounce) sour cream
1 egg, beaten
1/4 teaspoon almond extract
1 9-inch unbaked pastry shell

Topping:
1/2 cup quick cooking oats
1/3 cup all-purpose flour
1/3 cup packed brown sugar
1/4 teaspoon ground cinnamon
1/4 cup cold butter
1/2 cup pecans, chopped

In a large bowl, combine the sugar, flour, cherries, sour cream, egg and extract, stir well. Spoon this mixture into the pastry shell. Bake at 400° for 20 minutes.

For topping, combine the oats, flour, brown sugar and cinnamon in a bowl. Cut in the butter with a fork or pastry blender until the mixture resembles coarse crumbs. Stir in the pecans. Sprinkle over the filling. Cover the edges of the pie crust with tin foil strips to prevent over-browning. Bake 25-30 minutes or until the topping is lightly browned. Cool on a wire rack for 1 hour. Store in the refrigerator. Makes 8 servings.

Cherry Gelatin Ice Cream Pie

1 graham cracker pie crust
1 16-ounce can dark sweet cherries, pitted
1 3-ounce package black cherry flavored gelatin
1 pint vanilla ice cream, softened
1 cup whipped topping
1/2 cup almonds, sliced

In a bowl, drain the cherries saving the juice. Add enough cherry juice to make 1-1/4 cups liquid. In a saucepan, heat the liquid and dissolve the gelatin completely. Remove this from heat and stir in the ice cream until it is smooth. Refrigerate until thickened, about 10 minutes. Spread the cherries out on paper towels and blot dry removing any moisture. In the ice cream mixture, fold in the whipped topping, almonds then cherries. Spoon this mixture into the pie crust and refrigerate 3 to 4 hours or until firm.

Cherry Raspberry Pie

1-1/2 cups sugar
1/4 cup plus 2 teaspoons quick cooking tapioca
1/8 teaspoon salt
2-1/2 cups pitted tart cherries
1-1/2 cups raspberries
1 teaspoon lemon juice
pastry for 2 crust 9-inch pie
1 tablespoon butter

In a bowl, combine the sugar, tapioca and salt. Add the cherries, raspberries and lemon juice. Toss gently. Line a 9-inch pie plate with bottom pastry. Pour the fruit mixture into the pie pastry. Dot fruit with butter. Top the fruit with the remaining pie pastry, either a lattice crust or if you use a full top crust, cut steam vents in the top. Trim and seal the edges. Cover the edges of the pie crust loosely with foil. Place the pie on a foil lined pizza pan in a 400° oven for 30 minutes. Remove the foil around the pie crust and bake 5 to 10 minutes longer. Crust should be golden brown and filling bubbly. Cool on a wire rack.

Cherry Pineapple Frozen Pie

1 14-ounce can sweetened condensed milk
1/4 cup lemon juice
1/2 teaspoon vanilla
4 ounces whipped topping
1 cup crushed pineapple, drained
1/2 cup pecans, chopped
3/4 cup maraschino cherries, chopped
1 ready made graham cracker crust

In a medium bowl, combine the condensed milk, lemon juice and vanilla. Stir until well blended. Fold in the whipped topping, pineapple, pecans and cherries until well incorporated. Place this mixture into the prepared crust. Freeze for 3 hours. Before serving let stand at room temperature for 15 to 20 minutes.

Cherry Lemon Fruit Pie

1 graham cracker pie crust
1 21-ounce can cherry pie filling
1 8-ounce package cream cheese
1 cup cold milk
1 4-ounce package lemon flavored instant pie filling
1 8-ounce tub whipped topping

Spread 1/2 of the pie filling on the graham cracker crust. Then in a large bowl beat the cream cheese until smooth. Add the milk carefully and blend until smooth. Add the pudding mix and blend until smooth. Fold in 1/2 the tub of whipped topping. Spread this mixture over top of the cherries in the pie. On top of the pudding mixture, spread the remaining whipped topping and top with the remaining cherries. Refrigerate 3 to 4 hours. Serve.

Frozen Tropical Pie

1 14-ounce can sweetened condensed milk
1 12-ounce container whipped topping
1 20-ounce can crushed pineapple, drained
2 tablespoons lemon juice
1/2 cup ripe banana, mashed
1 large orange, peeled and sectioned
1/2 cup sweetened flaked coconut
1/2 cup toasted walnuts, chopped
1/2 cup maraschino cherries, chopped
2 9-inch ready made graham cracker crusts

Stir together the condensed milk and whipped topping. Fold in the next 7 ingredients. Pour evenly into the graham cracker crusts. Cover and freeze 12 hours or until firm. Remove from freezer and let stand 10 minutes before serving. Garnish with the fruits in the pie if you choose.

Bing Cherry Blueberry Pie

9-inch crust for double crust pie
1 cup sugar
1/4 cup all-purpose flour
1/8 teaspoon ground nutmeg
2-1/2 cups pitted bing cherries
1-1/2 cups fresh blueberries
1 tablespoon butter or margarine
1 egg yolk
1/4 cup milk

Line a 9-inch pie plate with bottom crust and set aside. In a bowl, combine sugar, flour and nutmeg. Stir in fruit. Let this set for 15-20 minutes. Mix well. Pour into crust. Drop diced butter on top of fruit. Top with pie crust. Seal the crust together. Beat 1 egg yolk and 1/4 cup milk. Brush this over the top of the crust. Sprinkle top of crust with sugar. Bake at 425° for 15 minutes. Reduce heat to 375° and bake for 30 minutes or until pastry is golden brown and filling is bubbly. Cool on wire rack.

Karen's Cherry Pie

From one of my best friends Karen Frampton.

Crust:

2 cups flour
1 teaspoon salt
pinch of baking powder
2/3 cup shortening
ice water

Filling:

2 16-ounce cans tart red cherries in water or 1-1/2 pound
*   frozen cherries, thawed, drained, reserving liquid*
1/3 cup cherry liquid
3/4 cup sugar
3 tablespoons cornstarch
1/2 teaspoon salt
1/4 teaspoon almond extract
1 tablespoon butter
sugar

Karen's Cherry Pie *Continued*

Crust: pastry for 2 crust 9-inch pie. Stir together the flour and salt. I like to add a little bit of whole wheat flour to my crust, with a pinch of baking pow-  der. Cut in the shortening and toss with a fork, adding ice water a little at a time, until it is just clumped up enough to form into two balls of dough. Roll out one half and place into a 9-inch pie plate, trimming the edge to 1/2-inch beyond the edge of the plate.

Filling: drain cherries, reserving 1/3 cup liquid. Combine the sugar, cornstarch and salt in a 2 quart pan. Stir in the reserved cherry liquid and cook until clear red. Add cherries and almond extract, mix. Pour into pie shell and dot with butter. Roll out remaining pastry. Cut slits or use a cookie cutter to design the top. Place the top crust over filling and trim the edge to 1-inch beyond edge. Fold top crust under the lower crust, form a ridge and flute the edge. Sprinkle crust with sugar. Bake at 425° for 15 minutes. Reduce temperature to 350° and bake 40 minutes more until crust is golden brown. Cool.

Pineapple Cherry Pie

8-ounces cream cheese
2 tablespoons pineapple juice
1/2 teaspoon vanilla
1/2 cup cherry pie filling
1/4 cup crushed pineapple, drained
1 8-ounce tub whipped topping
1/3 cup powdered sugar
1 baked 9-inch pie crust, cooled

Cream first 3 ingredients together in medium bowl with mixer. Add cherries, pineapple and mix. Fold in the whipped topping and powdered sugar. Spoon into cooled pie crust. You can spoon any remaining cherries and pineapple from the cans to decorate the top of the pie. Make sure the pineapple is well drained.

DESSERTS

*Whatever you choose to do will affect
everyone around you.*

Michael's Brownie Torte

Brownie mix
2 jars maraschino cherries, drained and chopped
1 large tub whipped topping
1/4 to 1/2 cup slivered almonds
1 small tub whipped topping, frozen or ice cream

Prepare brownie mix according to package direction, except bake in a round cake pan. Remove from oven and cool. Slice the brownie in half around the middle. Place 1/2 on a serving platter or cake platter. Fold the cherries into the large tub of whipped topping. Spread 3/4s of this mixture on the top of one brownie half. Top this with the other brownie half. Take the remaining cherry/whipped topping mixture and spread on top. Sprinkle the top of the torte with the almonds. To serve, slice desired portion and serve with frozen whipped topping or ice cream.

Good And Plenty Bars

1 stick unsalted butter, softened
1/3 cup granulated sugar
1/3 cup light brown sugar
1 egg
1 teaspoon pure vanilla extract
1/2 teaspoon baking soda
1/4 teaspoon salt
1/3 cup old-fashioned rolled oats
3/4 cup all-purpose flour
1 cup mixed diced fruit (cherries, apricots, apples)
1/2 cup shredded coconut
1/2 cup walnuts

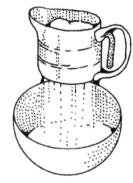

Preheat oven to 350°. Grease an 8-inch metal baking pan. In a mixing bowl with an electric mixer, cream the butter and sugars for about 5 minutes. Add the egg, vanilla, baking soda and salt. Beat at medium speed until blended. Add oats and flour, mix until well incorporated. Stir in the fruits, coconut and walnuts. Spread batter into the baking pan. Bake for 25-30 minutes or until golden. Let cool. Cut into bars and remove from pan.

Cherry Bread Pudding
From my mom Maryanne Manning.

12 slices white bread, french or cinnamon
butter or margarine, softened
cinnamon
1 10-ounce jar cherry jelly (1 cup) or cherry pie filling
4 eggs
2-2/3 cup milk
2 tablespoons sugar

Preheat oven to 325°. Spread butter or margarine on one side of each slice. Grease an 8 x 8 or 9 x 9 baking dish. Arrange 4 bread slices in the bottom of the baking dish. Sprinkle bread lightly with cinnamon. Place a spoonful of cherry jelly or pie filling on each slice. Repeat making 2 more layers.

In a medium bowl, with a whisk or fork, beat eggs, milk and sugar until well mixed. Pour over the bread and bake for 1 hour or until knife inserted in center comes our clean. Refrigerate. You can also serve warm.

Mom says using the cherry pie filling makes it more "cherry" and the cinnamon bread is very good.

Chocolate Cherry Tart

Crust:

1-1/2 cups chocolate cookie crumbs
2 tablespoons sugar
1/4 cup butter or margarine, melted

Filling:

1 cup sugar
1/2 cup butter or margarine, melted
2 large eggs
1/2 teaspoon vanilla extract
1/4 teaspoon almond extract
2/3 cup all-purpose flour
1 teaspoon baking powder
3 tablespoons cocoa
1 16-ounce can pitted tart water packed red cherries, well drained
1/2 cup toasted pecans, chopped

Crust: in a bowl, combine the crust ingredients. In a 9-inch greased and floured spring form pan, press the crumb mixture firmly into the bottom and 1-inch up the sides. Set the crust aside.

Chocolate Cherry Tart *Continued*

Tart: beat 1 cup sugar and 1/2 cup melted butter on medium speed with a mixer until smooth. Add eggs, vanilla and almond extract, beating well.

Combine flour, baking powder and cocoa in a bowl. Slowly add this mixture to the egg mixture beating until well blended. Stir in the cherries and pecans. Pour this mixture into the prepared crust. Bake at 325° for 1 hour and 10 minutes or until the center springs back when touched. Cool on a wire rack. Cover the tart and chill for 8 hours. Remove the sides of the springform pan. Slice the tart into wedges. Serve with whipped topping if desired.

Cherry Cookies

1 cup butter, softened
3/4 cup granulated sugar
3/4 cup brown sugar
2 eggs
1 teaspoon vanilla extract
2-1/4 cups all-purpose flour
1 teaspoon baking powder
1 package white vanilla chips
1-1/2 cups dried cherries
1 cup macadamia nuts, chopped

In a large mixing bowl combine the butter, sugars, eggs and vanilla. Mix until well incorporated, light and fluffy. In a bowl, mix the flour and baking powder. Slowly add this to the butter mixture until well incorporated. Take your mixing bowl and add the chips, cherries and nuts. Stir this mixture.

Preheat oven to 375°. Drop cookies by tablespoon onto your cookie sheets. Bake for 12 to 15 minutes or until golden brown. Remove cookies to cool on wire racks. Store in airtight container. Makes 4 dozen.

Cherry Soup

Soup:
4 cups fresh, frozen or canned red tart pitted cherries
2 cups water
1/4 to 1-1/4 cups sugar
1/4 teaspoon cinnamon

Dumplings:
2 cups all-purpose flour
2 teaspoons baking powder
dash of salt
1 cup milk

In a saucepan, put the cherries, water, sugar and cinnamon. Bring to a boil. Cooking cherries until tender about 15 minutes. Adjust sugar, if necessary to your taste and tartness of the cherries.

For dumplings, combine the flour, baking powder and salt. Stir in the milk. Drop the dumplings by teaspoonfuls into the boiling soup. Cook covered 10-15 minutes or until dumplings are fluffy. Serve hot. Makes 8 servings.

Frozen Fruit Mold

1 8-ounce can unsweetened pineapple tidbits
1-1/2 cups sliced bananas
1-1/2 cups seedless red grapes, halved
2 medium grapefruit peeled, sectioned and chopped
1/2 cup maraschino cherries, halved
1-1/2 cups unsweetened pineapple juice
1/3 cup lime juice

Drain the pineapple, reserving the juice. Place a banana slice in the bottom of each jumbo muffin cup. Divide the pineapple, grapes, grapefruit, cherries and remaining bananas among the muffin cups. In a small bowl, combine the pineapple juice, lime juice and reserved juice. Pour 1/4 cup into each muffin cup. Cover and freeze for 3 hours or until firm.

Remove from the freezer 30 minutes before serving. Turn muffin tin over onto a baking sheet to remove ice molds. Serve on small dessert plates. You can also put a popsicle stick in 1/2 way to 3/4 way of freezing and eat this way. Be careful of a "brain freeze" though. Great and refreshing on hot days.

Cherry Coconut Bars

Crust:
1 cup all-purpose flour
3 tablespoons confectioners sugar
1/2 cup cold butter

Filling:
2 eggs
1 cup sugar
1 teaspoon vanilla extract
1/4 cup all-purpose flour
1/2 teaspoon baking powder
1/4 teaspoon salt
3/4 cup walnuts, chopped
1/2 cup flaked coconut
1/2 cup maraschino cherries,
    quartered

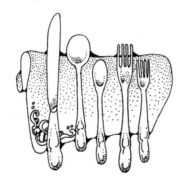

Crust: In a bowl, combine flour and confectioners sugar. Add the butter and cut it in with a fork until it is crumbly. Press into an ungreased 9-inch square baking pan. Bake at 350° for 15 to 20 minutes or until browned. Cool on a wire rack.

Filling: Combine the eggs, sugar and vanilla in a bowl. Combine the flour, baking powder and salt. Add the flour mixture to the egg mixture. Stir in the nuts, coconut and cherries. Spread over the crust. Bake for 20-25 minutes or until firm. Cool on a wire rack. Cut into bars. Refrigerate any leftovers.

Michael's Easy Cherry Brownies

1 package brownie mix
1/2 cup dried cherries
1/2 cup white chocolate chips
1/2 cup chopped nuts

Prepare the brownie mix according to package directions. To this mixture, fold in the dried cherries, white chips and nuts. Do not over mix the batter. Bake and cook as directed.

Cherry Pudding

1 quart cherries, drained
1 cup sugar
2 cups flour
1 cup milk
2 eggs
1 tablespoon butter
2 teaspoons baking powder

Place the cherries in a pie pan. In a bowl, mix the remaining ingredients well. Pour the batter over the cherries. Bake at 350° for 45 minutes.

Christmas Soup
A traditional Mennonite soup.

4 quarts plus 1/2 cup water, divided
4 cups mixed dried fruit
1 cup raisins
1 cinnamon stick (3-inches)
1-1/2 cups sugar
6 tablespoons cornstarch
1 3-ounce package cherry gelatin
1 16-ounce can pitted tart cherries, undrained

In a Dutch oven, bring 4 quarts of water, dried fruit, raisins and cinnamon stick to a boil. Reduce the heat, cover and simmer for 30 minutes or until the fruit is tender. Combine the sugar, cornstarch and remaining water. Mix well. Add this to the kettle. Return to a boil for 2 minutes stirring constantly. Remove from the heat and stir in gelatin until dissolved. Add the cherries and remove cinnamon stick. Chill, makes 3 quarts.

Black Cherry Mold

2 16-ounce cans pitted dark sweet cherries
1 envelope unflavored gelatin
1/4 cup water
2 3-ounce package cherry flavored gelatin
1 cup club soda or lemon lime type pop

In a bowl, drain the cherries reserving the syrup. Set the cherries aside. Add enough water to the syrup to make 2-1/2 cups of liquid. Bring the liquid to a boil in a small saucepan.

Sprinkle the unflavored gelatin over 1/4 cup of water in a small bowl. Let stand 1 minute. Combine the cherry flavored gelatin and boiled liquid in a large bowl. Stir in the unflavored gelatin mixture. Stir 2 minutes or until the gelatin dissolves. Stir in the soda. Chill mixture for 1-1/2 hours. Gently fold in the reserved cherries. Pour mixture into a mold if desired. Cover and chill 8 hours or overnight. Serves 8.

Cherry Crumb Bars

Shortbread Base:
1-1/4 cups all-purpose flour
1/4 cup granulated sugar
1/4 teaspoon salt
1 stick cold unsalted butter, cut into 8 pieces
1 egg white

Filling:
2-1/4 cups canned sour cherries, drained (reserve 1 cup juice)
3/4 cup granulated sugar
1/4 teaspoon salt
3 tablespoons cornstarch

Topping:
1/3 cup all-purpose flour
2 tablespoons packed brown sugar
1 tablespoon white sugar
pinch of salt
1/3 cup quick-cooking oats
3 tablespoons cold unsalted butter, cut in 4 pieces

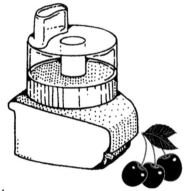

Cherry Crumb Bars *Continued*

Preheat oven to 350°. Line an 8-inch square baking pan with foil, letting the ends extend above pan on 2 sides.

Shortbread: process flour, sugar and salt in a food processor to mix. Scatter the butter on top and process just until a dough forms. Press the dough gently over the bottom of the prepared pan. Pour egg white over the dough and spread until coated. Pour off any excess egg white. Bake until golden brown 20 to 25 minutes.

Filling: bring 3/4 cup of the cherry juice, sugar and salt to a boil in a medium saucepan. Whisk cornstarch into remaining 1/4 cup cold cherry juice, then whisk into boiling mixture until the mixture thickens, boils again and turns clear, 3 to 4 minutes. Remove pan from heat and stir in the cherries.

Topping: process flour, both sugars and salt a few seconds to mix. Add the oats and butter and process a few second until evenly blended.

Remove the crust from oven. Turn the oven temperature to 425°. Spread the filling over the crust and sprinkle the topping over the filling evenly. Bake until topping is lightly browned about 25 minutes, then broil until topping is a slightly deeper brown. Watch carefully. Cool completely in the pan on a wire rack before lifting by the foil ends onto a cutting board. Cut in 16 squares. Remove from foil.

Simple Cherry Trifle

5 cups angel food cake cubes
1/4 cup cherry juice, optional
1 cup confectioners sugar
1 3-ounce package cream cheese
1 8-ounce container whipped topping, divided
1/2 cup toasted pecans, chopped
1 21-ounce can cherry pie filling

Place cake cubes in a large bowl and sprinkle with cherry juice. Let stand 30 minutes. In a medium bowl, combine the confectioners sugar and cream cheese. Beat this until well blended. Reserving 2 tablespoons whipped topping, fold in the remaining topping into the cheese mixture, stir. Add the pecans into the cake mixture, mixing well. Spoon cake mixture into a glass or crystal bowl. Spread the cherry filling evenly over the top or if you desire, a layer of cake, cherries, cake and cherries. Garnish with the reserved whipped topping. Serves 8-10.

Pudding And Cherries In A Cup

1 3.9-ounce package instant chocolate pudding mix
2 cups cold milk
1 21-ounce can cherry pie filling
2 cups whipped topping
maraschino cherries

In a bowl, mix pudding and milk according to package directions. Let stand a few minutes. Stir 1 cup of the pie filling into the pudding, then fold in 1 cup of the whipped topping. Using 6 glasses, divide half of the pudding mixture and equally spoon it into the glasses. Take the remaining pie filling and spoon on top of the pudding. Top the remaining pudding mixture and place on top of the pie filling. Garnish with whipped topping and a maraschino cherry. Yum! Serves 6.

Cherry Cream Soup

3 16-ounce cans pitted tart cherries, drained reserving the juice
1 cup water
1/4 cup sugar
1/2 teaspoon cinnamon
1/2 teaspoon allspice
1/4 teaspoon nutmeg
1 cup white grape juice
1 pint half and half or heavy cream

Chop the cherries and place in a medium saucepan. Stir in the water, sugar, cinnamon, allspice, nutmeg and juice. Bring this mixture to a boil over medium heat. Reduce heat and simmer covered for 5 minutes. Pour this soup into the serving bowl or a tureen. Slowly stir in the cream. Cover and chill until ready to serve.

Cherry Lemon Gelatin

1 3-ounce package lemon flavored gelatin
1 3-ounce package cherry flavored gelatin
2 cups boiling water
1 16-ounce can pitted dark sweet cherries
1 8-ounce carton lemon flavored yogurt

In a bowl, dissolve the two gelatins with the boiling water. Open the cherries and drain, reserving the cherry juice. Add enough water to the juice to make 1-1/2 cups liquid. Stir this into the gelatin mixture. Add the yogurt to the gelatin and beat with an electric mixer until smooth. Chill until partially set. To this, fold in the cherries. You can leave in the bowl or put into a mold and chill until set. Serves 8.

Cherry Chocolate Cookie Torte

1 pound package of chocolate covered graham cracker cookies, crushed
1 cup butter or margarine, melted
2 envelopes whipped topping mix
1 cup cold milk
1 teaspoon vanilla extract
1 8-ounce package cream cheese, softened
2 21-ounce cans cherry pie filling

In a small bowl, set aside 1/4 cup of the crushed cookies. Combine the remaining cookies with the butter or margarine. Spread into a 13 x 9 x 2 inch dish. Set aside. In a mixing bowl, combine the whipped topping mixes, milk and vanilla. Beat until blended, then on high for about 4 minutes or until thick and stiff peaks form. Add the cream cheese and beat until smooth. Spread over the crust. Top with cherry pie filling. Top the cherries with the cookie crumbs. Refrigerate for 12 to 24 hours before serving. Serves 12 people.

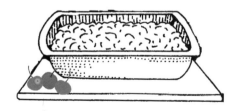

Fruit Salad Dessert

1 4 serving size package instant vanilla pudding mix
1/4 cup pineapple juice
1 8-ounce container whipped topping
1 cup pear, peeled, cored and cubed
1 cup fresh pineapple chunks
1 cup peaches, peeled and sliced
1 cup seedless green grapes, halved
1 cup canned pitted dark sweet cherries, drained

In a large mixing bowl, stir together the dry vanilla pudding mix and the pineapple juice. Gently fold the whipped topping into the pudding mixture. Fold in the pears, pineapple, peaches and grapes into the pudding mixture. Cover and chill for 4 to 6 hours. Just before serving, fold in the dark cherries. 6 servings.

Frozen Cherry Pineapple Dessert

2 8-ounce cans crushed pineapple, undrained
1 21-ounce can cherry pie filling
1 14-ounce can sweetened condensed milk
1 8-ounce carton whipped topping

In a large bowl, combine the pineapple, pie filling and milk. Fold in the whipped topping. Spread into a 13 x 9 x 2 inch baking dish that has been sprayed with a nonstick cooking spray. Cover and freeze until firm. Garnish with cherries and more whipped topping. Serves 12 to 16.

Cherry Cream Cheese Puffs

From my sister in Christ, Sharron Rockwell.

Cream Puffs:
1/2 cup butter or margarine
1 cup water
1 cup all-purpose flour
1/4 teaspoon salt
4 eggs

Cheesecake Mixture:
2 8-ounce blocks cream cheese
1 8-ounce container whipped topping
2 tablespoons lemon juice
1/4 cup sugar
1 teaspoon vanilla

Cream Puffs: In a medium saucepan, melt the butter. Add water and bring to a boil. Add the flour and salt all at once. Stir this vigorously. Cook and stir until the mixture forms a ball that doesn't separate. Remove from heat. Cool slightly about 5 minutes. Add eggs one at a time, beating with a wooden spoon after each addition for 1 to 2 minutes or until smooth. Drop batter by heaping tablespoons, 3 inches apart onto a greased baking sheet. Bake in a 400° oven about 30 minutes or until gold brown and puffy. Remove from the oven. Split, removing any soft dough inside. Cool on a wire rack. Makes 10.

Cheesecake Mixture: Beat all ingredients together until well incorporated with electric mixer.

Fill the puffs with a cheesecake mixture, top that with cherry pie filling and some whipped topping. Top with puff top and drizzle with melted chocolate.

Cherry Cottage Cheese Dessert

1 large box cherry gelatin
1 pound container small curd cottage cheese
1 large container whipped topping
1-1/2 cups dark pitted or sweet cherries, chopped

Prepare gelatin according to box directions. Mix all ingredients well in a bowl. Chill for at least 4 hours or until set. Serve.

Dessert Fruit Cups

1 to 2 medium firm bananas, sliced
1 8-ounce can pineapple tidbits, drained
1-1/2 cups pitted sweet dark cherries, sliced
1 can mandarin oranges, drained
whipped topping
coconut
slivered almonds

In a bowl, gently mix all the fruit. To serve, place in bowls. Top with whipped topping, coconut and slivered almonds. I like this served as a topping over vanilla ice cream.

WHAT NOTS

Love bears all things. 1 Corinthians 13:7

Peanut Butter Cherry Crunch
Michael's Recipe

1-1/2 cups powdered sugar
1/2 teaspoon ground nutmeg
8 cups rice square cereal
1 cup white baking pieces
1/2 cup smooth peanut butter
1/4 cup butter, cubed
1/4 teaspoon vanilla
1-1/2 cups salted peanuts or cashews
1-1/2 cups dried cherries

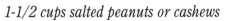

In a very large plastic bag, combine the powdered sugar and nutmeg. Set aside. In a large bowl, place the 8 cups cereal. In a medium saucepan, combine the white baking pieces, peanut butter and butter. Over low heat, stir these ingredients until melted. Remove from heat and stir in the vanilla. Pour this mixture over the cereal until the cereal is coated. Let this cool some. To the powdered sugar mixture, add the cereal 1/3 to 1/2 at a time. Shake to coat. Then add the nuts and cherries and shake. On a wax paper lined cookie sheet, place the cereal mixture. Cool. Store in an airtight container.

Frozen Fruity Yogurt
Michael's Recipe

1 cup pitted dark sweet cherries
2 8-ounce cartons cherry vanilla fruit flavored yogurt
1/3 cup honey or sugar
1/2 teaspoon vanilla

In a food processor or blender, blend the cherries until well chopped. Stir in the yogurt, honey or sugar and vanilla. Pour this into a loaf pan and cover. Freeze until firm. Break the frozen mixture into chunks. In a bowl, beat the frozen yogurt with an electric mixer until fluffy. Return mixture to a cold loaf pan and cover. Freeze until firm.

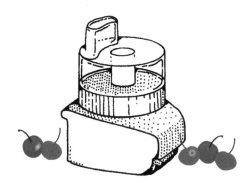

White Candy Bark
Michael's Recipe

2 8 to 12-ounce package white almond bark melting chocolate
1-1/2 cups cashew halves, almonds or pistachio nuts
1 cup dried cherries, chopped

Melt the chocolate per package directions. Stir in the nuts and cherries. Mix well. On a wax paper lined cookie sheet, spread out the candy mixture. Cool. When set, break into pieces and store in an airtight container in a cool place.

Yum Yum Snack Mix

1 12-ounce package chocolate chips
1 16-ounce package salted peanuts
1-1/2 cups round pretzels
1 12-ounce package white chocolate chips
1 12-ounce package vanilla yogurt covered raisins
1-1/2 cups dried cherries
1-1/4 cups cashews
1 cup pistachio nuts

In a bowl, mix all ingredients until well mixed. Store in an airtight container or Ziploc® bag.

Cream Cheese Fruit Sandwiches

1 8-ounce package cream cheese, softened
1 8-ounce can crushed pineapple, drained
1/2 teaspoon vanilla
1/4 cup dark red cherries, finely chopped
8 slices white bread

In a mixing bowl, stir together the cream cheese, pineapple and vanilla until well blended. Fold in the cherries. Divide the cheese mixture into 4 parts. Carefully spread the cheese mixture on 4 slices of bread and top with the remaining 4 slices of bread. You can trim the crust off the bread or use cookie cutters to cut in shapes. They make great tea time sandwiches.

Cherry Almond Fudge

2 cups (12 ounces) semisweet chocolate chips
1 14-ounce can sweetened condensed milk
1/2 cup almonds, chopped
1/2 cup red candied cherries, chopped
1 teaspoon almond extract

Line an 8-inch square pan with foil or wax paper (grease the foil). Set aside. In a microwave safe bowl, combine the chocolate chips and milk. Cover and microwave on high for 1 to 1-1/2 minutes or until chips are melted. Stir until smooth. Stir in the almonds, cherries and extract. Spread into a prepared pan. Cover and chill for 2 hours or until set using the foil or wax paper to lift the fudge out of the pan. Remove the foil, cut fudge into 1-inch squares. Store in the refrigerator.

White Chocolate Cherry Popcorn Balls

20 cups popcorn
2 cups sugar
1 cup water
1/2 cup light corn syrup
1 teaspoon vinegar
1/2 teaspoon salt
1 teaspoon vanilla
1 pound package of white almond bark
8-ounces dried cherries, chopped

Remove all of the unpopped kernels from the popped corn. Put the popcorn into a large roasting pan and keep warm at 300° in an oven. Butter the sides of a 2 quart saucepan. In the saucepan, combine the sugar, water, corn syrup, vinegar and salt. Cook to 270°, (soft crack stage) stirring frequently. Remove from heat. Stir in the vanilla. Remove the popcorn from the oven and slowly pour this mixture over the popcorn. Stir popcorn until mixed. To make balls, butter your hands and form balls. Make small balls, because they are easier to eat. Melt the white almond bark according to package direction. Roll the popcorn balls in the chocolate and then the cherries. Cool and dry on wax paper lined cookie sheets.

Note: you can use prepared popcorn balls and follow the directions beginning with melt the white almond bark.

Frozen Fruit Ice Cream Cones
Michael's Recipe

1 4-ounce container soft style cream cheese
1/3 cup sugar
1/4 cup sour cream
2 tablespoons lemon juice
1-1/2 cups pitted dark cherries or maraschino cherries
4 flat bottom ice cream cones

In a small mixing bowl, combine cream cheese, sugar, sour cream and lemon juice. Fold the fruit into the cream cheese mixture. Place this mixture in the flat bottom ice cream cones. Place the cones in a muffin tin pan. Freeze for 4 to 24 hours. You can decorate the cream cheese mixture with your favorite ice cream toppings before freezing. I like nuts on mine, Michael loves sprinkles. Makes 4 cones.

Easy Mix

1 cup pistachio nuts
1 cup honey roasted peanuts
1 cup dried tart cherries
1 or 2 white chocolate candy bars, broken into little chunks

Mix all the ingredients and store in an airtight container in a cool place, so the chocolate does not melt.

INDEX

Never underestimate the benefits of being a good listener.

Life's Little Cherry Cookbook

101 Cherry Recipes

Life's Little Cherry Cookbook